SHE STOOD IN THE
STORM

JOANNA FRANCIS

She Stood In The Storm

© 2016 by Joanna Francis

ISBN 13: 978-1539871392
ISBN-10: 1539871398

CONTENTS

DEDICATION

For my husband, Jon, and my children;
Josh, George and Beth, for always being there x

FOREWORD

By Cheryl Rickman

"She stood in the storm, and when the wind did not blow her way, she adjusted her sails."
Elizabeth Edwards

"We can't direct the wind, but we can adjust the sails."
Thomas S. Monson

So what are YOU going to do when the wind blows against you? Let it blow you down or adjust your sails? How are YOU going to deal with the deck of cards that you are dealt with?

Sometimes in life, you get thrown a curve-ball. Sometimes, that curve-ball is more like a roaring cannon ball. Either way, you can choose to let it knock you down and stay down, or, after it has knocked you clean off your feet, you can stand back up again and prepare yourself for another onslaught. The curve/cannon ball can take many forms. You might lose your job or a friend, your husband/wife might leave you, or you might face financial woes.

Or you might lose your health. Or your hearing. Or both. Like Jo.

This is the brave and honest story of my friend Joanna Francis who has weathered the most frightful storm(s), adjusted her sails repeatedly and set sail across unknown, frequently treacherous seas. Across the pages that follow she shares her dreams and her fears; her thoughts and her strategy for finding the stars amid the darkness.

I first met Jo when she was a teenager. That 15-year-old girl in her school uniform had no idea that, by the time she was 40, she would no longer be able to hear and would have battled cancer for eight years. That 15-year-old girl most likely couldn't have coped with that knowledge. None of us would. But then, that 15-year-old girl didn't have what the 40-year-old woman she has become *does* have – a rock solid armoury of enduring love and the stronghold of support that emanates from the depth of that feeling.

Over the past 20 years, ever since she met and fell in love with her husband Jon, Jo has been gradually throwing a log onto the fire of positivity that has equipped her to deal with the pain that she has endured. In positive psychology, scientific researchers call this the Broaden and Build theory – This theory says that, in experiencing positive emotions, our minds broaden and open up to new possibilities and resources, which can be drawn upon later in life, during difficult times, to enable resilience and boost well-being. So, each time we experience positive emotions we add to our well of positivity, which we can dip into during times of need. Conversely, negative emotions have the opposite effect, causing our minds to constrict and limiting our ability to be open to new ideas and connections, impairing our cognitive ability and resilience. As creator of this theory, Barbara Fredrickson puts it, "Just as water lilies retract when sunlight fades, so do our minds when positivity fades."

Jo has filled her well of positivity to the brim with love and laughter from her softly-spoken husband whose laugh soothes her; and the joy that being a mother to Josh (21), Bethany (17) and George (13) has given them both. Perhaps it is this that has helped her to cope with the unrelenting torment of a disease that has stolen so much from her? Perhaps she is stronger than she thought? Or perhaps, she, like so many others, has simply done what human beings often do when faced with incomprehensible adversity – continue – brave face on, head up? In this book, Jo guides us through her ups and downs during a snapshot of two years and shares the full spectrum of feelings from hope to despair and back again.

When Jo asked me to help her to co-write and edit this book, I said yes instantly, but I have a confession to make...I wondered whether I had the time. I was already juggling writing a couple of books and feeling a little overstretched. Then it struck me - time was something I am fortunate enough to have, that this incredibly wonderful, warm, kind and loving human being, my friend Jo, doesn't have as much of as she should. And that breaks my heart. But, thankfully, oh so thankfully, it does not suck the joy from the time she has. Conversely, and beautifully, it can, at times, magnify it, because time and moments become all the more precious and special.

As a friend of Joanna's, this is hard to write, but it is that feeling of uncertainty about the time she has left to spend with the ones she loves, which is the hardest part of what Joanna faces. And yet face it she does, bravely with grace. She knocks cancer out with a fist of pure love. And each time it comes back at her, which it has done time and time again, she stands up and faces it and knocks it out again.

So yes, I do have time. Most of us say we don't have time, but we do, unless we are facing the life-squashing time-thief of an illness like cancer, we have time. No matter how busy or time-starved you may feel, if you have your health, you are time-rich and it is up to you how you spend that precious gift.

We are busier than ever nowadays, but we can make time to do the things we cherish, somehow. None of us knows for certain what is round the corner and so we should do our best to find time, even tiny little pockets of it here and there, to do what we love with who we love. We should use those pockets of time wisely. And we should use our time to find joy.

This book, is not written to make people feel bad about how much they complain about life or how little they focus on what they are grateful for. (Permission to be human!) So, while it does help any of us who are blessed with good health to put our worries into perspective, it is meant to inspire us to find the joy in each moment, focus on the good and cherish what we have a little bit more, hug our loved ones a little bit tighter and embrace life a little bit fiercer.

For life is precious.
All life. Every life. Every moment.

Of course, joy is one part of the jigsaw of life. But so is despair. Life is like a roller-coaster for most of us. We all experience highs and lows, ups and downs. For some, the trajectory and duration of the downs are off the scale, but the ups still exist. It's a case of seeking them out. Sometimes it can be tough. Very tough indeed.

Over to Joanna...

CHAPTER 1

GIVE AND TAKE

WHAT IS IT ACTUALLY LIKE TO HAVE CANCER?

My sense of future has been taken away. I would love to grow old, but I shan't. I can't because I have stage 3B non-hodgkins lymphoma and that, my friends, is a pile of crap! It makes you feel like you're still part of the world, yet you're looking at that world through a looking glass, or from a distance; you are part of it, but not part of it. Your future has been removed. Seized from your grasp for no reason. Your life is no longer your own. You are forced to share your life with a nasty bedfellow; a rotten disease. How amazing it must be to remain blissfully unaware of your own mortality until the afternoon or evening of your life.

I've also lost my hearing through the process of this disease so in a goldfish bowl, peering through the glass is where I will stay. And this glass is most certainly not rose-tinted. One constant though is the ups and downs. That is the same for most of humanity. Some days are worse than others. Some days feel bright. Like hazy sunshine on a blue sky day, compared to the torrential downpour of the worst. The surgery, chemo and radiotherapy. The bad days, sad days, awful days. The days of despair when you wish so hard that you weren't creating so much worry and concern for all the people around you, for the people who love and care about you.

Equally though, believe it or not, there are great days too. Days filled with laughter. Like the laughs I've shared with family and friends over Christmas. My children and husband make me laugh until I can't breathe. You know, when your stomach and heart and cheeks and jaw ache all at once? I love that feeling!

Of course, the roller-coaster of emotions continues, as they do for us all. So yes, there are moments that have made me break down and cry over the past couple of days, like putting away the Christmas decorations and realising this could be the last time I do that. This is followed by a thought about how Jon will never wrap the fragile ornaments up as carefully as I do. Followed by a wonder about whether I will see the childrens' excited faces again at the beginning of the Christmas holidays as I produce their hot chocolate jars and allow them to watch Elf with me once more!

Traditions matter. I'm so glad we've carved them out. They can be continued. And, whilst they will be tinged with sadness, they will also act as triggers for fond memories and heartfelt moments in time. And nothing can ever steal those from my dear family. Nothing. Those are safe. And that is why making memories is even more important to me now than it has ever been.

Those closest to me now have genuinely realised that the subjects of our anxieties, all the stuff that we worry about on a daily basis – working to pay the bills, buying the latest gadgets and fashions, saving for an extension or a new oven – don't matter. No. None of that really matters. What does matter is finding your own happiness, spending time and making precious memories with friends and family rather than chasing money and material things.

That simplicity and clarity, that realisation about what truly matters in life – that is precious, but cancer is not a gift. However, if one person realises this truth about what matters as a direct result of reading about what's happening with me, I'll be a happy girl forever.

The fact that my own three wonderful children know this makes what they have had to go through less heartbreaking. Still heartbreaking that they must deal with all of this. I so wish they didn't have to. That they do troubles me more than anything I am going through personally. It's a high price for them to pay to have this insight. And yet, insight it is. Insight into what matters in life that they will take with them throughout their own. A shining gemstone of insight cracked open from within a sharp dark cold stone, which has caused them, and anyone it has touched, great pain. That's the only positive thing to come from any of this – the deepening of insight and the deepening of love.

GIVING

But don't get me wrong.
Cancer steals.
It takes away.
Apart from this insight and stark reminder about what matters in life,
cancer gives nothing, because, whilst it gives this insight with one
hand, it cruelly snatches life itself away with another.
It's brutal like that.

I will always want more time with my children and husband. It will
never be enough for me. I must teach them as many lessons as I can,
while I can, for as long as I can. And that is true for everyone, but of
course, I have not only the urgency to do it NOW, but also I have
no idea how long I have and will likely be debilitated in some form
until that time comes.

Yes, it's true, no one knows how long they have to live. But those
diagnosed with a terminal disease know what is most likely to kill
them. They know that their time is, not just going to be shortened,
but consumed daily with the treatment and effects of that disease.
It's not having a normal, healthy life that is relatively good and
healthy until a sudden accident happens. It's just not the same as
the general worries of growing older or aches and pains. It's never-
ending. I don't get to count down how many chemotherapy (or
other treatment) sessions until I'm done this time. Being done
will mean there is nothing left for me to try. Anyone who has
had chemo or radiation or some other type of therapy knows how
important it is to have an endpoint, a countdown. Knowing that
will never happen (and in fact, what you're really hoping for is a

lot of them, because that means you still have options) is one of the mental struggles each week, since it isn't just spending one day a week getting chemo, it's how it makes you feel each day after that. So yes, cancer does a lot of taking away.

Yet I think life is about giving, but not giving up. I am certainly not prepared to give up. And as this disease keeps taking, (my future, my health, my hearing, my job, even my two horses that I could no longer keep, because of my illness) I will do my best to counter that action by giving what I can.

I will do this as a mum, as any mum does. I will also do this by giving back to the charity that gave me support when I needed it the most – Wessex Cancer Trust (wessexcancer.org.uk).

They have helped me and my family so much, offering counselling and support. They are amazing!

Giving something back to them and my supportive family was my main motivation for setting up George Isaac Satchels, named after my youngest son, George. Prior to that I had sewed sock monkeys and contributed a percentage of profits to the Trust (25% of profits going to charity).

I had worked in a school as a teaching assistant and wanted to go on to be a teacher and use my degree in childhood studies. But I had to give up my job when I lost my hearing. Yet I didn't want to give up or sit on my backside doing nothing – I wanted to do something I could fit around hospital appointments and my loving family. Putting my talents to good use was the answer, as it gave me flexibility, and something to focus on while the children were at school.

I would have quite happily continued with my job as a teacher. However, after my diagnosis and losing my hearing, I had to give up a job I loved. With three children at school all day, I needed something to do. I decided to get creative and make my own version of the sock monkey. I wanted to tap into my skills of sewing and crafts, but I really wanted to give something back too.

I made a sock monkey for my son to keep him company whilst I went into hospital for an operation. He loved it, so I thought I could make these for other children too. And when friends asked me to make some for their children, I felt encouraged to take it further. Sometimes that's all it takes – the seed of an idea is sewn and then words of encouragement water that seed and enable it to flourish into an actual thing.

It felt wonderful to be able to use the sewing skills that my grandma had taught me at a very early age (and thank goodness she did)!

So, after making cushions and sock monkeys and then sweet trees for a while, I became too ill to continue. But I was reluctant to give up, so I launched forth with an idea I'd had for many years, but hadn't got round to putting it into action - George Isaac Satchels.

It was rewarding and demanding juggling being a mum with running my own business, (in between hospital visits) but it's been incredibly worthwhile giving something back and being my own boss and the flexibility that provides.

I would focus on learning about social media and promoting the business and answering emails in the evening and I'd dispatch satchels during the day.

My son George even got involved, doing a sponsored swim, and all of my children have been blackmailed (I mean persuaded) :-) to model the satchels for promotional photos.

Of course, running a business is not easy at the best of times, but I found it especially challenging getting the toys made and the satchels distributed whilst being very poorly. Sometimes it's really hard, but I have very understanding customers and I would even sew from my hospital bed. It inspired me that each toy I sold might bring a smile and cuddles to the person I sold it to, whilst also raising money for a worthy cause.

I learned a lot during my time as a business owner. Being organised was critical and I tried to under promise and over deliver whenever I could. I would still dream of having my own chain of sock monkey or satchel shops, for there is nothing wrong in hoping. Hope is stronger than fear. No, there is nothing wrong with hoping. And there is everything right with giving, so I will continue to give, for as long as possible.

Sadly, In January 2016 I had to make the decision to close the George Isaac Satchels website because, I wanted to shift my giving back towards my family and focus all of my energy and time on my husband and children.

I enjoyed making bags so much for so many wonderful people who have been such a great support on so many days. And yet, distributing orders and dealing with enquiries became too much as hospital appointments and days spent in bed became more frequent. Yet I didn't want to stop giving entirely. As well as giving to my family, I wanted to somehow continue to use my skills, as and when I felt up to it, without the constant pressure that running a proper online business entails. And that is how Tiny and Me came to fruition. I remembered back when my youngest was worried about me going into hospital for a big operation. I had made him a buddy who looked after my kisses and cuddles for him whenever he needed them.

Tiny and Me is a doll for a child going through cancer who can go through the same journey as the child. They have removable hair and also come with a hat or scarf. They are handmade from natural materials and have handmade up-cycled clothes. They also come with a book documenting the story so far but leaving room for the child to carry on their own story with their doll.

At this stage in my illness I can't do an awful lot, as I'm in bed a lot or at the hospital. That said, I can still sew.

The dolls for these children are free, but I will be selling dolls and also relying on donations to raise the money to cover the costs of the materials.

https://www.facebook.com/Tiny-and-Me-1722258434712103/

In teaching a child to be kind and give back we must lead by example. I am so devastated watching children on the news on a daily basis suffering in our world.

The only thing I can do, to give back, is to give away my dolls. Tiny and Me already give back to children suffering with cancer, but I want to spread this further.

Every doll I sell is raising money for me to donate a doll to a child in a hospital, orphanage or a shelter any where in the world. Hopefully, when someone purchases a doll, they can share with a child the value of giving back and inspire them with this small act of kindness. A toy can nurture a child's development, providing a much needed hug and comfort.

Tiny and Me - by being a friend and companion - also carries the message that, no matter where we live, what backgrounds we come from and how much or little we have; we can all be kind in the way that we live our lives; we can all give a little more.

HEALING

Talking of gifts. Nature gives. It's not surprising that the one thing that relieves my burning skin is natural and organic, whilst the chemical-ridden vomit-inducing radiotherapy is the cause of making my skin burn. Using high-energy radiation to shrink or reduce tumours is a treatment used by half of all people with cancer. But it's not pleasant.

Thank goodness for aloe vera!

Applied liberally straight after treatment, it really is delightful. A soothing treat amongst the treatments. What with the skin-burning radiotherapy and sickness that comes with chemotherapy, which makes you feel like you have heavy weights attached to each limb, everything feels like a struggle during treatment. But, after having your skin and body blasted with parabens and other irritants, the cool soothing powers of organic skin-saving aloe vera is so welcome and refreshing. Just wonderful.

Equally blissful are the holidays. Why do these holidays; these precious days to savour, whizz past so fast? Today is the last day and I intend to enjoy every single second. A crafting baking day with little G at his request. Quite honestly, I can't think of anything better. The oldest two are off out and, whilst G scrap books, I shall continue crocheting this cushion that I'm in the middle of (it's very bright, as I need some colour in my life)! I so love every school holiday. It makes my heart sing when the children are around, lazing about watching films. Together. Snug. It's been a cosy Christmas, as it should be. And today, I'm going to enjoy a beautifully simple, ordinary, delightful day.

It's on days like today when I feel so blessed and truly thankful for all that I have. Orders for satchels are flying in, so I have lots to do; plenty to keep me busy. I really want to develop my business this year and raise as much money and awareness for the Wessex Cancer Trust as I can.

Since writing the above blog post I am pleased (and a little bit blown away) to say I've somehow managed to raise thousands of pounds for Wessex Cancer Trust, through my sock-monkey making and satchel selling. And, although I've had to close the time-intensive online satchel business, I am now enjoying spending the days I feel well enough working on Tiny and Me – making dolls with wigs for children who need wigs.

I've had a lot taken from me – my hearing, my job as a teacher and my future. But it's important for me not to take offence at that.

"You either get bitter or you get better. It's that simple. You either take what has been dealt to you and allow it to make you a better person, or you allow it to tear you down. The choice does not belong to fate, it belongs to you,"

Josh Shipp

Rather, I want to give.

To GIVE this life my all;
to GIVE thanks for all that I DO have, rather than dwell on all that I don't or won't;
to GIVE back to the charities that have supported me and to those who need my support;
to GIVE as much of me to my children as I possibly can, for as long as I can.

CHAPTER 2

TIME AND JOY

I AM THE SUM OF MY EXPERIENCES

I will never know another day without cancer.

Like many of us I suppose, I also wish more than ever that I had the energy of my youth. I also wish I had the body, intact, fit and healthy. Good health. We take it for granted don't we?

Yet, would I want to tell my young self what lay ahead?
Would I wish to tell my young self to enjoy every second?
No I would not.
I wouldn't want to rewrite what has happened to me, because everything I have experienced has made me who I am today. Had I known my future, I may have made different choices and therefore may not be with my husband or have my three wonderful children; and those are what I am most grateful for in my life.

It's funny when I look back and realise things I thought were difficult to deal with have ended up being wonderful gifts from life. Although it's broken now, I'm so proud of what this body has done for me. My body has given me three beautiful healthy children. It's healed broken bones, battled infections and deals with my auto-immune disease. Right now, this body of mine is fighting an almighty battle with cancer. An enduring tiring battle, which goes on and on and has already taken so much from me. That's the ugly truth of this disease and, although I fight, it is admittedly taking its toll on me.

I know I will never ever be the same again.

So, I will never know another day of my life without cancer or treatment or dread.

That's a big realisation to deal with, but it is this fact which makes me more determined than ever to find joy in every day.

It hurts because it matters and it matters because it is good. So I am thankful that it is good.

I know some days that finding joy is harder to do than others as the fear and sadness get too much to bear. Enveloping me, crippling me, limiting me. And yet I do try and limit it back.

Yes, I have limited myself only a few minutes to give in to crying, as no good is ever going to come of that and, although it's important to accept our emotions and go with them, I want to make the most of all of my time. So I will continue on for as long as possible. No matter how long we have on this earth, we need to truly LIVE! All of our experiences contribute to making us who we are. The enjoyable ones and the terrible ones. We wouldn't be us without them. They are the segments of our lives that make us who we are. Whether we are feeling joy or pain, wonder or sorrow, we are FEELING, and that means we are living. Right here, right now, breathing in and out, making memories, creating experiences, developing relationships, carving out our life.

Learning, growing, being, feeling, loving, living……

REFLECTION

... And reflecting. As each year draws to a close we reflect on what we've learned, whether we've grown, what we have or haven't done. This time of reflection furnishes our dreams for the following years.

Yes, as the brand new year looms, of course, we are pushed to reflect on ourselves, to make ourselves and/or our lives better over the next 365 days.

Us human beings, especially ones living lives in this century at this time, we are on a journey. It's human nature to want to achieve. That said, change is a constant part of life and it's not easy to change habits and shift our thinking.

Still, we reflect on what we are happy with and what we wish to change.

We reflexively reflect on whether we've kept any of those elusive resolutions from the previous year. December 31st is supposed to bring a sense of "closure." In the arbitrary distinction between one year and the next; (after all, why is there really a difference between the last day of 2014 and the first of 2015 any more so than any other passage of midnight on any other day of the year?) yet we feel pushed to wipe the slate clean and start anew. And so we do.

And so did I. As I cleaned the house this week, clearing papers, clothing, and sprucing up the house I found I was instinctively doing this: "Out with the old, in with the new." This annual rehabilitation, then, is often both psychological and physical. Most of our resolutions are about ways we want to be better, inside and out: concentrating on the new and gaining closure on the past. "And yet, you can no more gain 'closure' on life-altering events than you can erase moments from your memory." This sentence is beautiful and true. No one really just sits alone and thinks about the tragedies that befall them. It's too painful, too powerful to take that in as one big gulp. Instead, what we do is weave it into the tapestry of our consciousness. We make it part of our daily life, quiet knowing, yet present.

Maybe, at this time of year, we reflect more than usual, and maybe that's why I find the holidays are as painful as they are joyful, because it's during this time of reflection that I take stock of what I've lost during the year and what I've gained. Where that balance lands says a lot.

A year ago I thought surely 2014 would be better than 2013? It had to be. Yet it really didn't turn out that way. Nonetheless, I am doggedly optimistic, even when I've been been proven wrong so many times. I do not believe that there is a "justice meter" in the Universe that is going to now dump things on someone else and leave me alone for a year. But maybe, as my own tapestry of consciousness continues to be woven, it will be stronger and more resilient in order to keep me going this year?

Today though, I can't help think of the things that cancer has taken from me. Stolen.

I am well aware of the blessings I have.
I remember them each and every minute of every day.

They are what keep me going, keep me fighting, but today, again, I am pulled into considering what's gone, what's irretrievable, what's changed for the worse.

It really is a balancing act – thinking.
Humans have a negativity bias. It's built-in.

Rick Hanson, neuroscientist and author of *Just One Thing,* says it best when he explains,

"The brain is like Velcro for negative experiences, but Teflon for positive ones."

Ultimately, we are wired to find it easier to ruminate on negative events and worry about our future than finding the good and focusing on thinking positively. Maintaining a positive mental attitude is tough. Especially when you have the sodding cancer cloud hanging over you. But that's not to say seeking joy and putting on a brave face is impossible. It can be done and it must be. Whilst I allow myself time to wallow and accept the sadness, I don't want to waste my time. I'd rather tip the thought scales towards the good ones and so I take a deep breathe and I notice all of that good stuff. I take note of it.

BECAUSE I CAN

I actually enjoy many simple things. I enjoy loading the dishwasher, bunging in a load of washing, cleaning the work tops and vacuuming around.

Because I can.

I walk the dogs on this summers day and I give my children an extra hug, an extra squeeze, just one more kiss, an additional "I love you" before they leave for school and college.

Because I can.

Yet still I worry about today, tomorrow, and the next day.
How can I not?
I put make-up and fake tan on yesterday. I can tell it put people at ease. If I look "healthy" they can relax. If I don't look sick, they won't have to worry how to act or what to say. And so they tell me, "You look good today."

Sometimes, it's true, I do feel good. I treasure those days like gemstones. Some days, however, just as the make up covering my face masks the severity of my illness, my brave face itself is a lie, and it's not how I feel. My face is not a mirror of my feelings.
Sometimes.
Some time.

I am grateful I have some time.
I am thankful for the kindness that gets shown to me every day by my family and friends.
For every email I get of support, every offer of help, every social event, every Facebook post;
For each photo, comment, and like, I give thanks.

But cancer sucks. This diagnosis is my nightmare.
I'm aware that tragedies happen to people every single day.
Lives are lost. I have learned of two deaths of friends' loved ones these past two weeks and I see the pain those losses have caused. There are no words to describe the pain of the people left behind.

Gone. A space where a person should be, now empty.
People live on in memories and are kept locked in our hearts forever.
But losing someone you love so deeply is beyond painful.
Not being able to cuddle them or talk with them or hear their voice.

Disease and death are heartbreaking for all involved. I wish that my life didn't have to revolve around this disease right now. So I do try to find some balance, to focus on giving and doing. I try to keep my life focused on others as much as I can. I see friends and family as often as I can. I try to keep up with the children (always a challenge) and I try to be a good wife and keep the house running. I wish I could be a better wife right now, but I do try to be strong and suffer on my own time. I try at these things, but I don't always accomplish them.
I try. And I try. And I try.

In trying I will never fail, because the only way to fail is not to try.

It's such an overwhelmingly isolating predicament. Few can know the anguish, the daily trials, all of the parts of my life which don't get shared with anyone. I share some here, of course, and with friends and family, but much of it is my own. And this is how it needs to be while I continue to process and make sense of this new chapter. It's the only way I know how to cope.

Thank you to you all.

JOY, MEMORIES & TEARS

I just want to see my son play basketball,
Watch him wave at me.

I just want to take my daughter shopping for make-up,
Applying powder to her porcelain skin.

I just want to laugh and joke with my eldest son,
Snuggled up in bed all together watching films.

How I love them.
I cherish this time; making memories.

I just want to grow old with my husband,
Continue to share our lives as we have for 23 or more years already now.
How I love him!

I just want to sit in the garden when we are old.
I just want to talk about the good old days;
To laugh and joke as we sit beside the fire.
Reminiscing.

›

I want to get a pedicure and have a nap in the chair.
I want choosing the colour of my nail polish to be the toughest
decision I have to make for a day.

I just want it to go away.
But it can't.
It won't.

I will never know another day of my life without cancer or chemo or
treatment or dread.

But I will search for joy.
I will.

I will do what I can every day to find that joy,
And if I can't find it I will make it.
This is my pledge,
This is my promise.
For them.

Some days it is hard to do.
Some days fear and sadness are too much.
Some days I do not know how I will do this with grace,
But I will try.

I must make the most of this time:
Helping others, educating, writing.
I know no other way to do this.
But it's the hardest thing to do.

So I do break and I cry, I give in to the emotions,
I let myself go and the tears flow, but only for a few minutes.
No good can come from that.

I gather strength.
I re-commit.
I go on living.

The bad days will come someday.

But that day is not today.
That time is not now.
And so I am a parent, a wife, a friend, a sister, a daughter, a writer,
and everything else I have been until now.
That is who I am.
That is who I will continue to be.

For as long as I possibly can.

CAKE AND BALLOONS

I am in limbo at the moment, waiting for results. Again.

I've been thinking about birthdays as a few friends have celebrated another turn of a number.

I watch them blow out their candles; what do they wish for I wonder? It's obvious what I would wish for.

Time with my husband.

Time with my children.

Time with my parents, brother and sister.

Time with my friends.

I wish I could go back to the time before I was diagnosed with this horrendous disease, ignorant and blissful. I have no way to know what or how everything will be when I reach my next birthday.

I wish for more chances and opportunities.

Chances for more memories.

Cakes and balloons.

Close your eyes and make a wish.

If only it came true!

HOSPITAL

There is something beautiful about the delicate unfurling of the morning, no matter where you are.

Do you notice that as you wake? The lightness? The freshness? The hope?

Even while I've been in hospital this week, I love it when the hospital inhabitants come to life for the day. Curtains are drawn and the sunlight pours in. Beds and pillows adjusted, IV pumps checked. Pills in plastic cups distributed. Velcro cuffs attached to arms, vials from my port and vital signs taken. Just before the doctors and consultants arrive and gather in suits to discover how your night went, the all important breakfast orders are taken, followed by a cup of tea and fresh jugs of water.

Then the real business of the day begins. Decisions about medication, chemo. Notes written, checked, updated. Decisions made. Will you go home or have to stay?

Each person has a life unfolding here today and it's important to remember, it is a life, not just a diagnosis or a body part.

Just because this disease can't be cured, doesn't mean there isn't a lot of life left in me, there is still so much for me to do.

I am living with cancer!
But I am living, nonetheless.

PAIN

Pain depletes us, whether it is physical pain or mental pain. We can't live our best life when we are in pain. We can shift our mindset to cope with physical pain and we can use tools and take action to calm and soothe mental pain, but pain can limit how deep we live our lives and dictate how we show up in the world. This week was a painful one as I returned to the Marsden to meet again with my doctors to reassess my meds and talk about the plan for the next few weeks.

Having recently suffered from pneumonia, I have to confess, on one occasion, I was quite frightened. Luckily for me, it's finally clearing up after a stint in hospital.

I owe a lot to the health care team. It's so important to form a team with your carers and focus on all side effects that you are having with all kinds of treatment. I've been in a lot of pain and, this alone takes its toll, not only emotionally but also physically. We function better when we are not weakened by pain. It takes trial and error sometimes to find the right drugs and also the right amounts. For me, for once, it all seems to be spot on! It can be distressing at times, but keep asking and with help from the team and unfortunately patience, peruse until a solution is found!

One interesting thing about pain though is this. Pain brings perspective to the times when you are not in pain. The relief you feel when the pain has gone or, at least, been controlled – that gives you a sense of appreciation that you wouldn't have without having gone through that pain.

Without the rain, there'd be no rainbow and without the pain, there'd be no relief.
Relief is a GOOD feeling.
Something to cherish.

Pain makes you remember that there is so much to cherish. Always.

We should try to make the most of every day.
Whatever that means to you, whatever you can do.
No matter how small it seems to you. Don't waste it.
We owe it to ourselves to delight in all there is to delight in.

One way to do this is to pause. Frequently.
To pause and savour. To soak up the good.
To cherish that. Take a snapshot of it. Store it in your memory bank.
And smile.

According to Barbara Fredrickson, positivity researcher and scientist, the more positive we are over time, the more resilient we are able to be in the face of adversity. It's like we store our positivity in a well of yayness that we are able to tap into when we most need it.

So when, like me, you have to battle an unforgiving vile disease that robs so many lives; live with the uncertainty of it and, simultaneously, live with what it has done to your body (for me, that is my deafness, as it stole my hearing six years ago)... you need a well of positivity that is positively over-flowing in order to avoid sinking down a well of despair; to rise above the anxiety and depression and hold on to those parts of your life that make your heart sing.

ANXIETY

Some days (and nights) are harder than others.
Sometimes I wake in the night needing something to calm my mind, when thoughts of my cancer progressing commandeer my brain. Over-flowing.

It is so very easy for your brain to get stuck in a loop of nervous anticipation, and, unless that loop is disrupted, your body will continue to be stressed.

For me, one of the most powerful remedies to my anxiety are my children. When I am really out-of-sorts, I connect with them and voila, I reconnect with the beauty of life, of love and of happiness. My children remind me that the world doesn't revolve around me – that there are far greater things to focus on and marvel at.

There are many things that can turn our attention.
It doesn't have to be children. It could be a friend, a family member, a lover; all we need to do is turn our eyes towards them. Focus on them. Find out what is happening in *their* world, see their beauty, and then we are freed from that loop of anxiety, stress, and fear. Even if only momentarily, it's important to punctuate the drama with some calm; to pepper the anxiety with some happiness.

So let us seek little pockets of joy within the minutes and hours and days that make up our lives. Let's not let those moments slip by as time passes. Grab hold of them. Savour them.

As Dr Seuss said, "Sometimes you will never know the value of a moment, until it is a memory."

The terror and dread of death forces you to cherish moments more. Fleeting moments take on a deeper importance. Life is for living, yet that term passes us by when we are getting on with the business of living our daily lives. So much so that much of our time is spent living rather than LIVING! When you know you have less life to live, living that life becomes more vital and has more urgency.

So whilst you do, at least at first, dwell and fall down the dark hole of depression and sorrow for that life. You soon realise what a waste of time that is. Nothing is going to change the outcome. We are ALL going to die one day. As each day passes we are closer to death, as morbid as that may sound. Time spent worrying, stressing, crying is time that you won't get back – once it's gone, it's gone.

So being told you are going to die sooner than you expected prioritises LIVING.

I didn't need cancer to tell me how wonderful life is, but it has made me value what I may have taken for granted for longer.

Of course, there is nothing good or helpful about terminal illness. I'd rather not have been robbed of my future. But I know I can use this to remind myself and others about the VALUE of life. The ideal would be to be healthy, and have a long guaranteed future and to appreciate life as much as someone who is having it taken away, so that you LIVE life to the fullest, without the illness, and you make the most of now. If you have that opportunity, why not seize it? Carpe Diem.

AND YET THE MORNING COMES

Each day is different. Each moment, too. It still seems surreal, this diagnosis of cancer. It's strange how quickly the horrific can become regular: the chemo, the side effects, the new routines. Oncology appointments, IV infusions, medication refills all start to fill my calendar. I start making lists of things I need to do. I prioritise them.

Top of the list is not always about what's actually the most important, it's also about finding things that bring me small moments of joy. The small moments are the ones that bring tears to my eyes. George mouthing to me, "I love you, Mama. You're the best Mama in the whole wide world" is enough to make me misty.

I still lose my temper. I still yell sometimes.
Often it's misplaced anger, a manifestation of my frustration with my situation. I haven't suddenly turned into the world's most patient person. Sometimes cancer makes me the most impatient one, in fact.
I feel the clock is ticking. I don't have time for nonsense.

But that's not a way to be. I will still try to be better. I try to be the one to do things with my children as much as I can. George and Beth always read to me at night for their homework: that is sacred. I still save artwork and photographs and remind them to brush their teeth and clean their rooms. I try to do the little things: helping with a school project, keeping company while she does homework, watching a sports practice if I can.

My motto is that I will do as much as I can for as long as I can.

I don't ever have a moment that I forget about my cancer.
I think that's the part about it being new. Even when I was diagnosed the first time — even after I finished chemo and surgery and all of it— it still took at least a year for me to be able to push the daily fear down.
Of course now the fear has been realised.
I am living it.
I am living my nightmare, one many people share.

And yet, the morning comes.
I see the light of day and I get out of bed.
I see the faces of my children.
I kiss my husband goodbye when he leaves for work.

Each day I have is a day that matters.
Each day is one to make a memory with my family and friends.
Each day is one more than I had the day before.

But let's be clear: there is no joy in this disease.
My appreciation for my days should not be interpreted as supporting the nonsensical idea that "cancer is a gift."

There is nothing positive about this disease; I would give it back if I could.
I did not need cancer to show me the value of things.
I always knew these things were true.
I never took them for granted.

I knew what demons could be lurking.

I did all I could maybe, just maybe, I can keep it at bay for a while.

I still haven't fully come to terms with what this diagnosis means, but that's because there's no real way to know.
We don't know enough yet.

It is the uncertainty that is the most difficult part for me.
Will this chemo be the one that lasts for a while?
Will it fail?
When?
What next?
How long will that one last?

My body holds the answers, but it's not showing its hand yet.
I have to learn to ride this roller-coaster. I'm just not there yet.
And I don't really know how long that is going to take.

I walk past people on the street and know they have no idea what is going on inside my body. Sometimes I want special treatment.
I want a Get Out of Jail Free card.

Most of the time, however, I want to stay home.
Hide out.
Be invisible.
I'm still processing. Reeling.
But while I'm doing that I'm living.

How many people wake up each morning with a real commitment to find the joy; seek the silver lining amongst the clouds and focus on being present instead of distant?

I suppose diagnosed people tend to. But what's holding every other healthy person from doing so?

Why wait to lose your health before you start living?

Annoyingly – when you lose your health you are often limited. But I'd rather make the most of the life I have, regardless of the limitations.

Finding joy amongst the pain becomes vital. Noticing the good becomes mission-critical. And, the knock-on effect of living in this way is a heightened sense of gratitude for what you have over what you don't or won't have. Focusing on what's going right instead of what's going wrong is medicine in itself.

CHAPTER 3

GRATITUDE

TO FIND JOY

I always find something to be joyful and grateful for, even if it's the smallest of moments each and every day. Today a lovely friend delivered the most beautiful bouquet of flowers, bright and cheery yellow. Just the sight of them made me smile. They now rest on my dining table.

I have my special comfy chair in my dining room, where I like to look out at the trees, watching with my heart full as their leaves move in the wind. The birds perch on the branches, singing joyfully; what beautiful life exists in my garden.

There is a shimmer in each and every day. I know that some days we have to look hard for it, dig deep. Some days there is just a darkness that looms overhead, foreboding, especially when waiting for results, like I currently am for a scan.

Yet I find that writing my blog, shedding light on this journey and giving a voice to those depths is important.

And so I shall always search for joy. I have made a promise to myself that I will do what I can everyday to find that joy. No matter how difficult it sometimes is.

Occasionally, the fear and the sadness are overwhelming and become too much to bear. On those days I'm not sure how I will do this; but I promise to myself to always try.

A GLASS HALF FULL NOT HALF EMPTY

I spend a lot of time, so much time, inside my head: the silence, the twisting, the pulling and the ruminating. This, however, does not mean I'm sad. I'm just thinking.

I've made mistakes, (who hasn't) but I don't look back and regret things, because doing so is a waste of precious time. I learn from them, but I don't regret them.

I want my children to look at me and think, although ill, I have lived and made the most of life.
I don't give up. I just will not.
I want to go out in this world and participate in it.

Many years ago, I had to give up my beloved job, teaching.
Working in our local school with wonderful children and wonderful staff made me feel incredibly happy. I woke up everyday looking forward to my job. My work energised and engaged me. It gave my life meaning, just as being a parent does. It brought me so much joy, I was so happy teaching.

Yet, things change.

I had to rise to the occasion or sink under sheer sadness that almost overwhelmed me.

After a few months, sewing, making sock monkeys and sweet-trees and trying different activities to earn a living whilst giving some profits to charity, George Isaac Satchels was born.

Because I made a decision when things changed for me.
I decided this. I am not going to sit and just have cancer.
I want a job, I want to work, and so I created one.

How exciting and what a joy to have our own bag line that enabled me to raise money for our wonderful charity, the Wessex Cancer Trust.

You can shut yourself away (and believe me, not doing so is hard) or you can take charge of your life and fight fight fight.

When cancer and other diseases try to destroy you, to seize control of your body, you can accept that and roll over and give up, or you can refuse to let it take complete control; you can focus on the areas that you still have control over – your thoughts, your appreciation of what you have, your actions, your relationships, your drive, your will.

I want to succeed.
I want my business to raise as much as it possibly can.
I want my children to always have an attitude of a glass half full, not half empty and that is what I have to nurture.

We will only make it under these circumstances and not through locking myself away.

I get such joy from being a mother, a wife, a daughter, a friend. I am in control of those relationships, of how I parent, how I nurture, how I push forward. So I will continue to do my best!

GIVING THANKS HAS BEEN LIFE-GIVING

I am so thankful to be surrounded by love from my three amazing children and wonderful husband, family and friends. This unforgiving disease may have robbed me of my hearing, but it has not and never shall rob me of my spirit nor the gratitude I feel each day for what I have.

Every day, while I of course experience moments of deep sadness, anxiety and despair, I make sure to also focus my attention on being thankful for all that I have. I choose to focus on that. Naturally, being human, my thoughts drift towards the unfairness of it all, to whether this Christmas could be my last, especially when I battle with tiredness and sickness from another bout of chemo, but then then I seize back control by considering all that I have got, rather than all that I haven't.

This gratitude and the constant love of my family is what has helped get me through tough times and enables me to bounce back and make the most of each moment of my precious life.

There are bad days, sad days, awful days. Days when you wish you weren't creating so much worry and concern for all the people around you, for those who love and care about you, but, believe it or not, there are great days too. I have had loads of laughs with my family and friends. My children and husband make me belly laugh until I can't breathe.

Giving thanks is giving me my life life back by reminding me what I still have right now. As such, gratitude is incredibly powerful and comforting.

A stack of scientific studies have been carried out on the topic of gratitude, revealing how gratitude is good for health and well-being. These studies have revealed that counting your blessings and focusing on what you are grateful for makes you a better friend, student, partner and even parent. Appreciation is good for the heart, according to the American Journal of Cardiology, and the immune system too.

While gratitude is not a cure for cancer, depression or any disease, it has been scientifically proven to help make people better equipped to deal with what life throws at us on a daily basis. By practising being thankful with committed regularity, we can boost our positive emotions and, in doing so, bolster our resilience so that we may make the most of each day. That is what I try do do and, in doing so, I hope to teach my children and friends to do the same.

NEW YEAR'S DAY

Home is where the heart is. And today, home is where it's at. As the rain pours down in sheets and the wind twists and turns outside, home is the best place to be.

We've all enjoyed the snuggly comfort of home after the night of celebration welcoming in a fresh new year. Sometimes, being at home feels like the greatest luxury; drinking tea, eating chocolate and watching films with the children.

How lucky we are to live at little206.
Bliss.

WAIT. HOW DID WE GET HERE?

"How did we get here?" I asked my love, across the bed strewn with childrens' gadgets, crochet and a book.

"We got here because of your amazing strength, commitment, and love for your family that you have shown since you were diagnosed, almost seven years ago," he replied.

Since that fateful day, life has been one non-stop adventure.
Non-stop.
A perpetual roller-coaster.

I nod.

"And because of you, always at my side, supporting me, joking with me, taking me to yet another appointment and holding my hand… kidding me about the speed I drink the shakes, and raising eyebrows with me as the nurses hands jiggle as she tries to place the line."

I smile.

"No matter what, you deserve to feel better right now," he adds, squeezing my hand.

"You deserve to enjoy family and friends, or go to the moon.
We will make as many of your dreams come true!"

And so we do.

I truly, madly, deeply love my husband.
He is my rock, my soul mate and the person I love for also giving me
my three wonderful children x

With him by my side I feel grateful beyond measure.
For I have love, and am able to give love, and live loved.
And isn't that what life is all about?

POSITIVE MENTAL ATTITUDE

Snug.

The weather has been pretty atrocious, but, on the plus side, we've all spent a huge amount of family time at home together. It's been so cosy and relaxing.

We are still firmly in holiday mode and I'm going to struggle to let go of that feeling. Morning lie-ins have followed late nights. Chocolate croissants with films for breakfast and not a uniform in sight! I have enjoyed our Christmas break so much!

Daylight has seemed to be in short supply here. This wet grey weather makes it feel as if we are moving from dawn to dusk with nothing much happening in between, except for grey murkiness. The days are short and dark, but that doesn't stop the light.

Indeed, another pleasure is lighting lots of candles and enjoying their cosy glow.

Warmth.

With all the Christmas decorations packed away into their various bags and boxes and the tree now banished from the house, everything is looking a bit more like normal.

I did so miss the smell of the Christmas tree as I came downstairs in the morning. That comforting scent made me smile and feel contented, so I would breathe it in deeply.

Content.

Everything is now cleaned and dusted down and the task of preparing school uniforms and work shirts must begin! Although apprehensive, for obvious reasons, I have really enjoyed the heading into a New Year.

I love the upbeat feeling of new beginnings, fresh plans.

I am stepping into 2014 with hope and excitement.
My husband and I spent quite a while chatting about all that we want to achieve together, with the children this year, and so PMA, as my friend always says, Positive Mental Attitude!!

We are ready x

THINGS TO BE GRATEFUL FOR

I think the key to finding peace during difficult times is to monitor negative thoughts or fear.

Try and remove any thoughts that dwell on the past or project into the future. After all, we can't change the past and we don't know what will happen in the future. Far better to focus on the right now; on this moment.

As I myself am currently living with cancer, this personally comes up for me quite often. Days, even weeks before my scans, blood tests and cancer markers, I know that worrysome thoughts are simply unhealthy and useless to aiding my health, since I have absolutely no control over what the future holds. One thing I know for sure: Worrying about it will not change it and will not make me feel better, only worse.

I cannot afford to have my mind ruin my joy of being here. Yet, of course, like everything in life, this is easier said than done!

Therefore, I have decided that, before going to bed, I shall look back over the things that have made me happy each day. I have taken to writing them down or capturing whatever I am grateful for by taking a picture; whatever I have been grateful for from the day, however small. This simple process helps to calm my mind.

One of the things I have been grateful for today is my slow cooker, which I have rediscovered. It's a lovely feeling to come home from the school run, open the front door and smell the dinner cooking away all by itself. Marvellous!

I am also very truly grateful for my husband and children and where I live.

Also, being deaf, my dogs are very precious to me, as they keep me feeling safe when I'm alone during the daytime.

The power of the mind is an amazing thing and it can be both a healer and a slayer; negative thoughts can be replaced by healthy thoughts and beliefs.

I feel that, if I can control my thoughts, then I have more control over my life. I can adjust my own sails and steer my own ship, to a certain extent. This is obviously vital for me. Really, it makes sense that the only thoughts worth thinking about are:

- love of self
- love of others,
- love of life.

When I practice this, I truly begin to create a sense of well-being.

Cancer, like any life-altering experience, cracks each one of us to the core. That crack, however, holds the potential for us to reassess our priorities and make each choice, each moment, each day count!
There is so much in life that we have absolutely no control over. Like disease. But then there is so much in life that we can control. Like love.

Like our thoughts.

Like how we choose to respond to the stuff that we can't control.

So surely we owe it to ourselves to focus on those few things within our control, rather than the multitude of things outside of it?

In life, we cannot control the cards we get dealt. Yet we do have a choice about how we choose to play those cards.

I choose to be grateful for what I have, rather than to focus on what I don't have, won't have or can't have.

I choose to focus on the good. That's a conscious choice that I choose to make each day.

This is a useful way to handle any adversity – be it loss of health, a loved one, a job. Find the good; seek out the beauty. This is how I deal with the cards I have been dealt. A good friend of mine who has lost both her parents chooses to focus on how grateful she is to have had both of them as her parents. As she says, frankly, she could have had crap ones. But she didn't. She focuses on what they gave her rather than what she has lost.

(Obviously, there are times when we cannot bear the pain and we crumble and weep and falter, but we need to give ourselves permission to be human during those times; accept those feelings, let it all out, and then seek out the beauty and the good and rise up again despite it all). For others, who've lost loved ones I have heard how they have focused on seeing the beauty in all the good work they did whilst they were here and how they chose to live their life, making the most of it.

One thing I know for sure is that there is always something to be grateful for, even during the darkest times. There is always light. It's just a case of looking for it and holding on to it; grasping that torch to reveal the way forward, onward and upward.

For me, I am most grateful for my children and my husband. They are my world.

MY CHILDREN

Every time I look at each of you, my heart could burst. You are all so very deliciously different, bringing so much joy to my life. You each give me so much strength, you make me fight and you make my heart swell with pride!

I wish I could be with each of you every day, I want to know everything and not miss a thing. I'm so truly proud of each of you.

Being your mum is just the best experience in the world. I love being your mother. You are my world.

I know you carry a burden of having a poorly mum, but the way you each deal with it on a daily basis just has to be admired.

The way you each love and care for, not only me, but each other, makes me feel so comforted.

You have had to grow up so fast and deal with your own adolescent lives as well as my cancer.

You support, you care, you listen; we laugh until our sides hurt and then we snuggle.

Sometimes I think to myself how strange life is.
You're given something with one hand and then it is taken away with another. Yet, I suppose it's all about balance.

I have been blessed with such an amazing family, such amazing children that, although cancer has arrived at our door, I can still have amazing days. I am still blessed, because I have you. That is more than enough to bring me daily joy. Having the three of you as my dear darling children.

I still haven't fully come to terms with what lies ahead, but that's because there's no real way to know. It is always the uncertainty that is the most difficult part for me.
Will this treatment be the one that lasts for a while?
Might it fail?
When?
And what next?
How long will that one last?

Uncertainty generates questions questions questions!
My body holds the answers, but it's just not showing its hand yet.
And so we continue on, together, loved and loving, cared for and caring for.
Waiting, wishing. But always in each other's hearts and minds.

To my dearest children,

Someday you will understand the depth of my love for you.
Perhaps it might take until you are adults, perhaps made more vivid if you are fortunate enough to have children of your own.
No matter when, no matter how,
I hope you will someday learn this powerful emotion I feel for you.

You give me strength.
You make me fight.
You give me joy.
You make my heart swell with pride.

I want to see it all.
I want to see every day.
I want to know every phase of your lives.

My darlings, let me tell you something I take such pride in: ... YOU!

Parenthood is a lifelong commitment.
There is no backing out, changing your mind, saying "it's too much."

I adore and am honoured being your mum.
Your flaws and your talents make my heart soar in equal measure...
they are what make you who you are - YOU.

You are each so different, so unbelievably deliciously divine in your
own way.
Never doubt that my heart bursts every time I look at each of you.

I'm pouring every ounce of love into you that I can.
I'm going to just keep doing it every day.
Being your mum is the best thing there is.

Thank you.

I LOVE YOU TO THE MOON AND BACK

Some days I could cry a river.
I wish so desperately that things were different.
But no. I concentrate and stop myself.
For what good would that do?
It won't take this disease away.

So I put my hand in yours and I feel safe.
Love is a very powerful thing like that.
It generates warmth and safety and hope and strength.
You give me strength.
I'm so grateful for you.
You stand by me and I can feel brave.

I want time to slow down.
I want the days to be longer, to deliver me some hope!
I don't want this cancer to be my headline news, I want it in the background
of my life, not being in the spotlight, which it seems to crave.

Yet this is the way it is.
Everything the wrong way round, upside down.

But first things first.
I may be a cancer patient.
But I am a wife, a mother, a daughter, a friend FIRST.
And, above all else, I love you to the moon and back x

TEARS OF FRUSTRATION

I am so blessed that I am able to experience motherhood.

This is why, on days that I have had enough of cancer, on days where I think 'no more', I just look through the prism of motherhood and realise there is still so much to see and do; to feel and experience. The emotions of motherhood are incredible. I don't have to look very far to be filled with such overwhelming love for right here right now. All I need to do is just look into my childrens' eyes!

Some days I am so desperate not to think or talk about anything to do with cancer. But, unfortunately, it is part of the new me. It's hard not to feel defeated when it just seems the mountain is so big to climb. The summit seems so high and far away to me.

Right now, we are making a change with treatment to try to get better results in controlling cancer progression. This cancer doesn't give a damn about my family or anything that matters to me. It's ruthless. So all we can do is our best to regain control over it. Thank goodness for doctors and nurses, because they do care. They continue to show care and concern and they work so hard to try to make things better. Without them I simply would not be here.

I do shed tears out of pure frustration, although I try to not let that happen too often.

I'm not sure I can ever properly come to terms with what is happening to me, although I have accepted that this is how my life is going to be, and that now I have a constant companion (enemy) that I am going to have to learn to get along with.

That is just the way it is.

And that is frustrating and heart-breaking.

We shall continue to do our best, and let the medical profession do their best, and I will do what I do best — give love to the important people in my life. For that gives me comfort. A comfort blanket to calm the flames of frustration that flare up from time to time.

MOMENTS BECOME MEMORIES

I stand outside with my arm linked in my dad's and I pause for just a moment.

The realisation that all my friends and loved ones, including my future husband, are within the church dawns on me. And I feel a wave of nervous excitement all rolled up into a wonderful ball of joy and happiness. I just cant wait to see his face!

Here I go. This is it!

The sun beams down on my face. I can still remember the warmth of the day. I'm so pleased that I stood and savoured that one moment in my life, absorbing what I could see and hear and feel. Because, now, I can transport myself there whenever I like. All I have to do is close my eyes.

My story isn't all one sided, as my husband stands right beside me every single day. We have grown up together and shared so much. It's been an honour to spend my life with him.

When I said my vows, "in sickness and in health" of course I meant every word I said and when he said those words to me, little did we realise just how big a promise we made to each other that magical day.

My dear husband has shared everything with me through this painful journey that we find ourselves on. Every appointment, chemo, radiotherapy, blood tests, check ups, scans.

He has shared in the laughter and all the tears.
The pain and the heartache.
He is such a kind and caring man. So thoughtful. He works so hard.

Marriage is more than I ever thought it would be.
But what brings the most delight are the small acts of kindness, the thoughtfulness, the talking, respecting, laughing.
Those are the things that matter.

Those are the experiences and the qualities that I cherish.
Thank you husband of mine.
You mean everything to me.
I find strength in our union.
United we stand; facing the world and the hand we've been dealt, together.
In love. In sickness and in health.

CHAPTER 4

THE FUTURE

HARDSHIPS

Hardships can be soul-destroying, but equally soul-strengthening. They may break it but then they strengthen it. Academic studies and military training suggest that the strongest teams are formed through shared adversity. So, although we never want our family to have to endure anything difficult or painful, if we have to battle through a shared adversity, we do grow stronger as a unit. I can testify to that.

But of course, we do our best to protect our children from everything.

I so wish my children didn't have to deal with this... and yet I can't change the past or the future. It provides me with some comfort when I hear all the incredible stories of people who have been through incredible hardships, tragic circumstances and faced insurmountable loss, yet who have used these awful experiences as springboards to propel them forward - to make a difference in the world, to change the status quo, to achieve great things, to make those they have lost proud, or simply to show up in the world as the best versions of themselves. And so I know that, awful as the pain and heartache that my family face, it will ironically somehow serve them in their journey through life, both should they become parents themselves and out in the world of work and love and relationships and all. They will grow and develop into better people because of their life experiences, not despite it.

I want to protect them from pain, but it is true that what doesn't break you makes you stronger. Loss leads to pain, but pain leads to resilience. From darkness comes light. And without the darkness, you wouldn't appreciate the light so much. And I have to say, my children are so appreciative and brave and thoughtful. They amaze me every day. Those who have been through hard times often bounce back and become the best version of themselves.

One thing I know for sure. My children appreciate so much. Their eyes have been opened to such difficulty and pain and yet, this has helped them to be grateful for what they have and to cherish the moments we share. I know in my heart of hearts that each of my children are incredible people. They will each do well in their lives and they will always be kind and loving to others. I am so very proud of them.

I wish they hadn't had to go through any of this.
I wish life had been easier for them.
But I can't take any of it away.
And so I hope that they can take these adversities and thrive by putting what they've learned about life into practice.
Learning, growing, and experiencing the joy that they all deserve.

I can't change the past or the future. I can only impact this moment. So I give all I can. I know that one day I won't be here to guide them and hug them, but I will always love them. Love never dies. And I hope that I have given them enough love to fill their hearts for their entire lifetimes. I will live on in their hearts and will always be a part of them. Forever.

A DIFFERENT FAMILY UNIT

From my bed, from the other side of the patio doors, I watch my family in the pool.

My husband dives in, followed by the children. Their faces appear in the water, my husband takes some strokes and splashes my youngest. They race each other; leaping in and out of the water. My three children float, bobbing in the pool.

Suddenly, at this moment, I feel the distance between us and it feels like a lifetime. It is my beautiful family in the pool floating away from me.

I see them, the quartet, and I watch as an outsider.
I do this a lot lately.
I watch them from afar and think how it will be without me.

I can't help it.
A new family unit.

Behind big black sunglasses, my tears stream down my face.

Before long, George, my youngest is running from the pool to me.

He stands, dripping, face beaming.

"I just wanted to tell you I love you, mama."

I take his picture.
I capture the moment.
I grab him, hug him, feeling the cold water on him, melting in to my hot skin.

I whisper to him what a gorgeous boy he is and how much I love him.
And then I send him back to the pool, away, so I can cry harder.

By the time they get out, I'll have composed myself.

And yet, my daughter immediately senses something amiss.
"Are you okay?" she mouths to me.
And pantomimes tears rolling down her cheeks.

"Yes," I nod.
I walk out to the poolside to prove it.

People with terminal illnesses often wonder what life might be like for their loved ones after they are gone. It goes with the territory. One day I won't be here to stroke their hair and remind them that they are safe and loved. But my love won't stop. Not ever. I hope that is of some comfort to them. I hope that they know the depth of my love. And I hope that will spur them on to achieve their heart's desire and continue to be the incredible humans that they already are.

Nobody knows what the future holds. All we can control is how we respond to each moment that we experience. If we focus too much on the past (on what we had, and have lost) or on the future (on what we have, but may lose) the current moment would be tainted with what ifs and whys, instead of joy and gratitude and love and awe. It's a waste of life if we make the choice to focus on the past or the future.

When I left school and got a teaching job, I had no idea that my illness would put an end to the teaching career that I loved so much. When I left school, I had no idea that I would have cancer and would be robbed of my hearing and of my chance to grow old. Of course, that is why each person on this earth should do all they can to make the most of their every moment in this life. None of us know how many moments we shall have to enjoy.

So let's enjoy as many moments as we can. Let's savour the present, rather than reflecting on the past or worrying about the future.

Because we have that choice.

We can choose to shut the curtains and the doors and hide away from the world. Allow the darkness to swallow us up. And in doing so lose the moments and all that we still have. Or we can choose to live each day; to focus on the good, to focus on being a mum/daughter/dad/son/friend, to live in the moment and embrace life, warts (or cancer) and all.

A LEAP OF FAITH

Talking of the future. When your future is uncertain, it takes a lot not to think about it. It takes a lot not to make plans or to be brave and go ahead with making plans anyway. It takes a leap of faith every day. There is a leap that comes when you think to yourself each night, "The world will be here tomorrow, and I in it." Statistically, it is likely to be so. But what about the day after, and the day after that? How many days do you think ahead?

I wanted to buy plane tickets for a dear school friends wedding but I cannot. I think to myself, will I take another trip away? But how can I think of my life in 15 months time? It scares me to think what it will be, what will I be? So, I cannot.

I do talk of taking holidays next year with family. I do believe I will be alive.

(And guess what... two and a half years after writing this particular blog post, I returned from a truly wonderful holiday to Croatia with my family, which was such a tonic. Yes I'm awaiting more test results and yes I'm very poorly, recovering from a recent op, but 30 months after writing this blog post, here I am, living and loving.)

Of course, the fear lingers and niggles around what the quality of my life will be like in the months that follow this one. What chemo or radiation or surgeries will I have needed by then? And what regime will I be on and how will I feel from it?

Just being alive is not always enough. Because life is about living not existing.

I didn't buy those tickets, but I do still think the thoughts.

One of the hardest things I have found is that I feel I cannot make promises, because I don't want to cancel. And so I don't promise. No guarantees. I'm forever saying, "Let's play it by ear," "Let's see how it goes," Because to plan, to get hopes up, to think it could come true...then to have those hopes dashed would just be too hard for me. I don't want to let people down.

The thing with incurable cancer is, I can't have the confidence the suffering will end because it is temporary. It is not temporary.

I do keep pressing forward though, in my own way:
With strength, with dignity, and yes, still with great hope for more time.

Sometimes I wonder if it is that hope which buys me more time?

And yet, often times, many days, that is one of the hardest things about it all: I can't just mark the time and get through. Knowing the hardest parts will soon be over. Because I know the hardest parts are yet to come.

NUMB INSIDE AND OUT

I keep trying to move forward.
Sometimes I'm crawling.
Sometimes I'm marching.
Sometimes I just need to stop to rest and take note of my location and my surroundings.
I'm numb inside and out, but I'm determined.
I'm always grateful, always hopeful,
But God knows I'm often melancholy.
I wish I could put more distance between it and me.

CHAPTER 5

FEAR, THOUGHTS AND WISHES

FEAR

I know I'm lucky.
This may seem like a strange thing to say, given my reality, and yet I know that I am.
I have been blessed with many things and I will always be thankful for that.

Some days though, feelings overwhelm and burst the river banks of my mind. They flood me, like raging seas and, just like water, they seep into everything I do.

Those feelings of fear then affect my mind and body.
Today is one of those days.
I have to talk to myself constantly.

One half of my brain is emotional, irrational; the other half sensible and mature.
I have to force myself to talk to the emotional irrational part of me with compassion, and talk myself round.

I wonder though, why do some days contain all these emotions?
Why am I stronger yesterday compared to today?

The one emotion I don't like is fear!
It's a particularly crippling emotion.
Fear makes every movement difficult, until the sensible side of my brain kicks in and saves me.

"There is nothing to fear," says sensible brain.

"Enjoy right now, cherish this very moment, savour it. Don't think about even an hour ahead, rather, absorb this moment in time. Go on!" it tells me.

"Talk to your children, throw yourself into now, because now is what matters."

The sensible, mature side of my brain calms me for a minute as I listen.

As I breathe deeply, in and out. Slowly. In, 2....3.... Out, 2...3.... I know this is exactly what I should be doing! And breathe.

Over thinking and blowing my fears up like huge balloons is something I can do very easily; we all can. Neuro-science tells us that humans have this negative bias. It's just the way our brains are built, which is why it doesn't take very much for our worries and judgments and fears to spiral out of control.

That's why looking for the good in each moment, even during times of adversity, and savouring every positive moment is so important.

Of course, sometimes, it's almost impossible to do this and you can sink under a wave of despair. At times like these, being deaf becomes overwhelming. These are the times I yearn to hear my husband's soft voice, to hear his calming words making me feel safe (thank goodness he has strong arms for cuddles). These are the times I feel desperate to hear my children, their laughter. Oh, their laughter! These are the times when I long to put on some music; to just disappear into the song that understands everything you are feeling and thinking about, the kind of tune that, by the time it's finished, you feel so much better!

But no. I've been robbed of my hearing, so getting through these days is much harder to do. The quiet makes the darkness darker, the thoughts louder and yet, without sound.

But before I succumb to the darkness, I need to pull myself out of it. I need to do something to reconnect with normal life; a walk, a simple walk, even though it is raining; a walk to breathe in the fresh air and clear my head.

However, the bigger question for me is how are we, as humans, supposed to battle these trials? How do we make these trials our weight bench instead of our cement boots?

I need to focus on what I was created for, my purpose in life, and not on that which I can no longer do. This is likely to lead me up a path of less fear and anxiety and help me spend more time focusing on the happiness and well being of the world around me; to focus on what I was put on this earth to do.

Just like an athlete training hard for the Olympics, I call on my inner strength and my sense of purpose to push my body and mind toward hopes and dreams, accepting and using that which I was created for to overcome hurdles no one has yet reached.

We all need to dream big, to use what we have to live fully and treat each day like it's the best day of our lives!

The darkest hour is before the dawn.
And life is precious and wonderful and there to be enjoyed and savoured and cherished.

Until the next time when the wave of fear rises up and we make the choice to breathe, to focus, to find the good and choose life.

SOME DAYS WHEN I WAKE

Some days when I wake I don't feel like doing much, going anywhere, wanting to do this.

Some days when I wake I don't know how to get out, or want to be the brave one, be the strong one.

Some days when I wake I don't understand quite how I got here, care to see where it is going, even want to imagine what it will be like after.

Some days when I wake I don't have any words, or the strength to take them from my head and put them on a screen.

Some days when I wake I don't believe this is what my life is, what it has come to, or even think I have woken up for the day.

Some days when I wake I don't wish to believe the best days are over, know if the adventures have ended, want to believe that it can be true that they are.

But even on the days I don't... somewhere inside, I know I must press onward, for whatever that means, for right now.

So every day, that is just what I do.

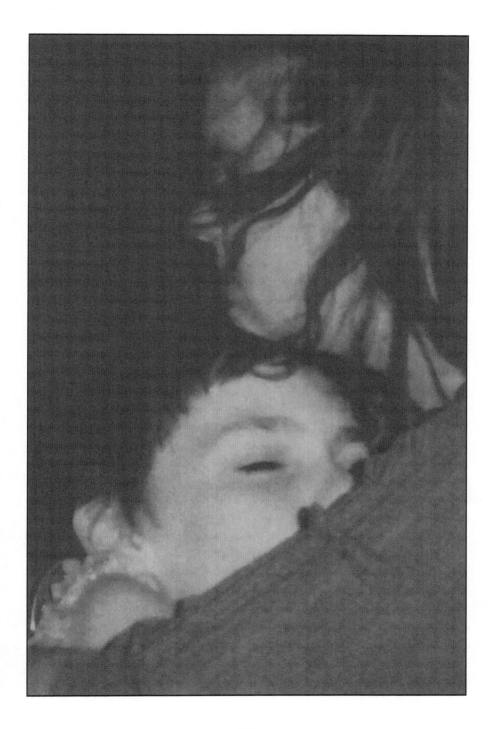

MUM, ARE YOU SCARED?

One night each week, the children and I have a snuggle night.

My husband works long hours, so it's a night of talking, laughing and drinking hot chocolate. I love our snuggle nights. We've never let our children sleep in our bed, so they think climbing in is a big treat. I asked them if they wanted to talk about what was going on. They did as they normally do. My youngest always gets distraught with me being deaf. He cannot bear that I am unable to hear his voice. It torments him. He is learning to play the saxophone and he struggles with the fact I can't hear him play, but I love to watch. He seems to be absorbed with his instrument. My heart squeezes!

This time though, my daughter asked me a question.

"Mum, are you scared?"

I told her that yes, I was scared. I explained that my fear usually comes from the unknown, from the uncertainty, in this case just how I will respond to treatments. I told her it was okay to be scared, that it's normal. I explained how sometimes fear makes you brave enough to do things you don't think you can otherwise do. She asked questions about genetics - what her risks of getting cancer would be, then they asked about what kind of treatments I might need.

My youngest gets terrified of me having chemo. He didn't cope well when I lost my hair and became bald. He became very protective of me. He would hate leaving me alone, especially when he went off to school, so, whenever we embark on something new, he panics.

My daughter asks me again, as if to confirm for herself, "It's not curable, right?"

I tell them that sickness can be scary, but I don't want any of them to be afraid.

My youngest son wants to be a doctor. He wants to know about all of my surgeries and the treatments I've had. He wants to know how all the medicines and treatments work and he knows every pill I take; how many and at what time of the day.

My daughter asks how we will know if treatments are working? I told her how important it is for me that they live their lives. How I want our house to be as normal as it can be for as long as it can be. I told them that they should try to focus on their school work; on their sports, their music and their friends.

I told them that what we were doing in this moment, lying here together talking about this, was the most important thing we could be doing today.

I told them, like I do every single day (about a hundred times) that there isn't anything more important to me than my family.

My job is to help them deal with this, whatever this is, and that what my daughter might need from me would likely differ from what her brothers might need. Each of them will have different needs along the way. It's my job to figure that out and address it. For my husband, too. How I take the lead on this will be important. How I choose to react and how I help them cope with how they react.

We talked on and on as I combed my fingers through my daughter's long curly hair; as I stroked her smooth, soft cheek.

My children give me strength.
Love is powerful like that.

TERRIFYING JOURNEY

Life. We are here now in the present moment and yet we spend a lot of time thinking about the past and thinking about the future. Reminiscing and reflecting, worrying and pondering. Forwards and backwards; backwards and forwards. It can be difficult to pull ourselves back from the past and back from the future to the present moment of now.

And this is the problem.

It's a slow terrifying journey creeping through the numbers of the different stages of cancer.
Your sentence changing with a number.

One of the things that bothers me the most about this disease is the knowledge that the way I feel right now is likely the best I will ever feel for the rest of my life. It's only going to get worse, right? That thought terrifies me.

Many years have passed since being told that I have cancer and so my journey with this alien on board my body then began, back then, on the first day that my life would change completely; taking a different path than the one I had imagined.

I think back to the days when I could hear. I travel back into my past.
I miss the sound of my children's laughter.
I wonder what they sound like now?
I miss the comfort of my husband's voice.
I miss being able to to talk to my friends over the phone.
I miss the things we take for granted, like going out in a group and being able to understand the whole conversation.

I miss the days that started innocently, normally, benignly.
I think of what I achieved before all this happened.
My life as it was then.
My career working in a school.

I ponder about where I have been, where I am now and, the scariest of all, where I am going?
I picture the amazing people I have met along the way, wonderful new friends, the doctors who work so hard to save me and the nurses who work just as hard, but also take the time talk to me.
I think of my friends who have died from cancer since I was diagnosed.
My friend who was taken so quickly. The day she held my hands and said, 'Jo, I'm so scared!'

I think of the progress I've made and the distance I have yet to go.
I think of what today might bring, and tomorrow.
And then, I stop.
I stop myself from thinking too much.

My thoughts have travelled backwards and forwards, to a past I cannot change and a future I cannot know. Only now can I control how I feel, what I do, how I live.

And that is what I must do.
"Don't dwell," I tell myself.
"Go live your life."

Thinking is good, but only so much.
Doing is better.

HOW CAN I HATE THAT WHICH GIVES ME HOPE?

I feel alone.
Willing myself to recharge, gather strength, get ready, be stronger.
My chemo starts again in one more week.

My relationship status with chemo on Facebook would read:
It's complicated.
However the chemo keeps me alive. It's this amazing drug, which buys me time and gives me days, weeks, months. But oh it makes me sick. Causes my hands and feet to numb, get tender, peel, redden, swell, ache, burn, throb.

Chemo tires me like nothing else, sickens me and weakens me.

How though can I hate that which gives me hope?!

I check in with friends on Facebook. I see the photos of beautiful people in amazing places doing things I want to be doing. I then feel that ugly emotion of jealousy and it makes me cry. I literally weep at the beauty of a friend, just wishing I could be with her, with them, anywhere but here. I cannot now decide if in this stage of cancer I must downsize my dreams or shoot for the moon.

I dream of New York city. A place I want to see on a crisp winters day with beautiful, brightly lit Christmas trees. To walk in Central Park with my family by my side. Wistful I remain. I'm unsure I will see that place now*. I envy those who are there. They will never know how I envy them.

*Note: I wrote the words above in September 2014. The very friend who was visiting New York, which made me long to be there, which made me fear that I might never be able to do so, she is helping me write this book. And guess what? I made it to New York City. Over a year later in December 2015, my family and I travelled to New York for my 40ᵗʰ birthday. And what a treat it was! It's hard to put it into words.

My concern about whether I might ever see this place was unfounded. Because I did it.
I got to achieve my dream of going to New York.

And so it served as a reminder that there is always hope; that time spent worrying about what might or might not be is time wasted.

Dwelling on the past and worrying about the future are normal human activities, but it's the stuff that is happening in the present moment that has the most power. Sometimes these are good experiences and sometimes bad, but it's up to us to choose how we react to them. And it's not always easy.

DO THINGS HAPPEN FOR A REASON?

Do things happen for a reason?
I'm not sure if they do any more or if it's more about how you respond to things, that really just happen.

When these astronomical things occur in your life, I find you have to make a conscious decision and decide how you are going to handle it; how you are going to react. For, in the end, it is your response that gives you your power, it is how you respond which either gives you hope or despair.

As a mum, one of the hardest things for me to deal with is trying to protect my children from the pain. You try to protect your children from all types of pain as soon as they are born. That protective instinct is paternal. It's just what you do as a parent.

I have done everything in my power to insulate them from the pain they are all in now. To try to take the edge off it. The hardest part is knowing that I am the cause of distress.

However, my actions, my responses, can teach lessons: important ones. I can grow, get stronger, and choose things that I otherwise never would have.

Alternatively, you might learn that you made a mistake and should deal with a situation differently the next time it comes up.

Everyday I talk to myself and I make a conscious effort to try and stay upright and not collapse under the emotional and physical pain of this cancer. I can't believe that there is a purpose in suffering, so saying that things happen for a reason suggests this was given to me and designed for me, which I find hard to rationalise.

Is this all part of some grand plan?
Will all this lead me onto something bigger and better?
Will enduring this pain in some way benefit my children in the long run?

Who knows? One day I or they will find out, but for now my conscious effort to keep going remains the same, whether this was meant to happen for a reason or not. It is what it is and I will do what I can to respond as well as I possibly can to this card I've been dealt.

I can respond with resentment and bitterness and sadness. I can respond with hope and tenderness and resilience. I can respond by focusing on all that is good in my life. I can respond by showering my children and husband with every ounce of love that I have to give. I can respond by taking time each day to do the things I love to do. I can respond by giving back, by being kind and by fighting hard. And so I shall.

THE LOSS OF MY HAIR

At times I feel stripped of all dignity. I don't feel feminine any more, let alone human. That feeling was never stronger than when I started to lose my hair.

I had long dark hair. I've always had long hair. Even when I was younger.

Before school, I would get up in the early hours and give myself at least an hour just to attend to my hair and no one was allowed to touch it! Needless to say, losing my hair was a tough one for me.

It terrified me to wake to find clumps of hair on my pillow. Running my fingers through my hair, just touching it, to feel strand upon strand falling out. I woke up one morning to discover a whole handful of hair resting next to me. It actually made me physically sick and I shook uncontrollably.

I felt ashamed and embarrassed in front of my husband and so scared to see my children. I dreaded to look in their eyes and see the sadness and fear. I remember my head feeling so hot and itchy.

Then there's the eyebrows and eyelashes, nasal hairs. WOW, how important are they? I didn't quite realise the importance of those little hairs and so, yes, a runny nose I endured.

It felt to me at this point like layer after layer was being peeled away from my whole being.

After a while of clumps of hair falling out, I decided to go for the chop. I didn't even do the whole gradual, have-it-in-a-bob-and-get-used-to-it-short thing. I sat in the kitchen with my children holding my hands and my husband shaved the rest off.

And the strangest thing happened. For that moment I felt empowered, because we took control.

Although copious amounts of tears were shed, we did laugh at how funny it was that I now had less hair than my husband. As usual, my family were there holding me up and giving me strength to get through.

And this is one of the many reasons I raise the money I do. The Wessex Cancer Trust provides an invaluable source of information and they have an amazing team of people all working to aid people like me through these tough times. They provide counselling, advice and even complimentary treatments to just give you that help, space and time out, so desperately needed from this horrendous disease.

They help give people some control, and feeling an element of control during times of uncertainty, taking back control over what is happening to your body is helpful.

I AM BALD

There. I did it.

Here I am taking chemotherapy.
Eyebrows almost gone.
Eyelashes disappearing.
Maybe I'll try pencilling them both in to hide their absence.

I don't have many pictures of myself bald.
Now I'm sporting the jelly baby look, this will be my one picture to document it.

I had just stopped crying. Long enough to put on make-up and try a smile. Of course it's run of the mill for doctors and nurses to see people bald. They see cancer patients all of the time, but, for me to reveal my naked head; it's another way my dignity, my identity, my humanity is being stripped from me. I don't like people to see my head. Somehow it's more personal, more private, more embarrassing to me than anything else I have to go through.

When the doctors or nurse see my baldness, there is embarrassment there, because it's not happening on my terms.

So today I am taking control and doing it on my terms.
I see ladies at the hospital wearing no head scarves or wigs and I think to myself that they are strong. They are real. They are brave and also they are beautiful.

I bet it feels liberating to them.
So I'm trying it.
I'm taking off my scarf and going bald here today as I want to see how it feels.
There, I did it!

I am bald, but I am bold!

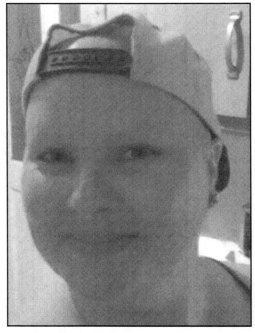

ARE YOU READY?

I have a confession to make.

I have a terrible fear of being unprepared. I wake up in the night gripped with panic and fear, because of this disease. I even panic as I'm walking around the supermarket. Suddenly I'm consumed and overwhelmed with fear because of this disease. My hands go sweaty and my breathe quickens.

Uncertainty is quite terrifying. It's a tough state to inhabit. It can be unbearable and it is often the uncertainty of situations that leads us to feel most anxious.

None of us can know exactly what the future holds, even if we've been told that our future won't extend for as long as we had hoped it might, we still don't know what will happen day by day, until it happens. This makes it difficult to prepare. Equally it gives us the freedom to enjoy the present.

Some people hope for the best and visualise that and others focus on the worst so they won't be disappointed if they were right. I don't want to be negative, and yet I want to be prepared, because of this fear of not being so.

Perhaps this fear has been magnified because, the one time I wasn't worried was the one time I got it wrong. When I went back for my second scan I wasn't concerned– in the least. There was a small lump, but it didn't worry me at all, and when they kept taking pictures, I wasn't worried. When they did the ultrasound, I wasn't worried. When the technician called in the radiologist to look at the ultrasound images, I wasn't worried. When they took me into a separate "discussion room" I still wasn't worried.

But then the radiologist said the words that I wasn't prepared for, the words that scared me, the words that were devastating. It's as if the words she said weren't in my vocabulary, therefore, when I saw what she was telling me… "it's probably cancer…" I had no reflex in place to catch me as I fell.

Here I was, unprepared in every way to digest the news.
You just don't think it will happen to you.
When it does, whether you expect the worst or hope for the best, it's all irrelevant, because nothing can prepare you for that news.

Still, at that point, all I knew was that I never wanted to experience that shock again.
From that moment on I was fixated on preparing for what lay ahead.
I didn't want to be unprepared any more.
Never again.
Because being unprepared was unbearable.

I walked through the world in a blur for that month while decisions were made.
My body shut down and I was anxiety-laden.
I knew I needed to make a plan.
In getting a plan I would feel empowered. I would regain control, and that I did.

Once my decisions were made about surgery and adjuvant therapy, (chemo and long term hormone therapies) I think I became resigned.

I needed to know what to expect.
I needed to know what I might be able to do to take care of my family and how to carry on during what would likely be one of the toughest physical and emotional challenges of my life.

When my hair started to come out in clumps from the chemo, my husband took the clippers and shaved my head.

I needed to take back control. Expecting the worst or hoping for the best was no longer relevant – staying in control in the moment was. It helped me to feel prepared for whatever I might face.

I know you can't control it all and I don't have the energy to worry all the time.
But I also know that, in being prepared I am self-soothing, trying to reassure myself that things will be okay.

I'm not sure I believe that yet. It's a daily struggle. But I learned my lesson by dropping my guard. As a student of life, I failed once.
I won't do it again.

I feel prepared for good things to come my way and I brace myself for the bad. I strive for balance between hope and acceptance and I focus on the present as much as I can.

Control what I can.
Be prepared for what I can't.
That's as far as I am right now.

WORRY

At the Royal Marsden we've been watching my tumour markers and we aren't quite sure what to make of them. They have been rising a lot in the past month, but I am also getting varied results. I have a scan coming up and, of course, this is the key piece of data to look at. It's been a challenging few weeks emotionally for me as I see where the markers are. I stare without blinking. I watch them rise and I wait for the scan to tell me what's truly going on inside by body.

Hopefully, over the next few weeks, I'll have answers.

I've been given a new drug, which is like a miracle for me. Although this disease continues to develop inside of me, the good days are almost out-weighing the bad at the moment. That's been unheard of for a long time.

So I continually try to bring my focus back to the distinction between worrying and planning.

I have realised that worrying is essentially devoting a large amount of time thinking about things that may or may not happen.

Charlie Brown once told Linus, "Worrying won't stop the bad stuff from happening. It just stops you from enjoying the good."

Worrying about the results is not going to do me any good. The cancer is doing what it is doing. Worrying won't stop that, but it will stop me from enjoying my life right now – moment by moment.

Planning is different.

Taking strategic action to set things in place and control things that I can control in the midst of so much uncertainty. That's helpful.

Which reminds me of the Serenity prayer:

"God grant us the serenity to accept the things we cannot change, the courage to change the things we can, and the wisdom to know the difference."

Having a backup plan or a next step, if and when the scan brings bad news in the next week or so, is planning. That helps me to feel more prepared and, ever since the thunderbolt through my heart in 2008 when I was told the news that I had this disease, I am keen to control what I can, accept that this is happening and plan accordingly.

The drugs I take, which I am truly grateful for, are either working or they are not. My sadness or frustration about that won't change the reality of the processes.

And so I have been quieter this week, choosing carefully how to spend my time.

I'm searching for joy each and every day and finding beauty in the small moments. Walking my dogs, doing home work, shopping with my children, eating out, watching films, enjoying coffee with my dear friends.

In my family we hug a lot.
We say "I love you" a lot.
We have always done this.
But now I hold on for an extra second each time and I squeeze just a little tighter.

SOMETIMES

Sometimes doing everything you can is not enough.
Sometimes your best isn't good enough.
Sometimes things don't work out the way you want.
Sometimes it just isn't fair.
Sometimes the end comes too fast.
Sometimes time won't slow down.
Sometimes your plans won't happen.
Sometimes those dreams won't come true.
Sometimes your life feels like a nightmare.
Sometimes nightmares happen in the day.
Sometimes uncertainty is a needy child that won't leave your side.
Sometimes there isn't enough strength.
Sometimes it's more than you can handle.
Sometimes the end is near.
Sometimes there isn't anything you can do.
Sometimes staying strong isn't an option.
Sometimes a word or gesture or deed can bring you to tears.
Sometimes strangers show the kindness that should be shown by ...
Sometimes you can't see which way the road will go.
Sometimes all you can do is research, then close your eyes and guess.
Sometimes strength may look like denial;
Sometimes you must trick yourself to get through the day, or hour, or minute.
Sometimes the reality is so unfathomable you must push it aside.
Sometimes the pain is too great.
Sometimes people don't understand.

Sometimes they make what's hard even harder.

Sometimes the kindness of friends makes things bearable though.

Somehow the strength of love can keep you going for a while.

Sometimes you get lucky.

Sometimes you don't.

Sometimes what happens has nothing to do with you.

But somewhere, deep in the darkness, you must hold out hope.

THE CHAIR

As I wait for an appointment, I often wonder, how many people have sat in this very chair before me? Each and every person has a story and I always think about this chair's story too.

I think about how many times I have sat in this same place; how many years have gone by and how much I have changed since I first sat here.

Then there is the chair in the consultant's room.

How many people have sat here and had their lives flipped upside down and changed forever, just as mine has. I've sat here as a new patient and now as an established patient. I've received both good news, and devastating news. I've gone through treatment plans and scheduling of more scans and tests.

Sat here in this chair, I have felt so many emotions. As this is the chair I sat in to be told for the first time " you have cancer".

And then, "it's back."

I have felt shock and disbelief, denial and grief, anger and frustration.

I've felt sadness and numbness and loneliness, right here on this chair.

I've sat in this chair with long hair and no hair, feeling depressed and tired, sick and in pain.

In this chair, I've asked the questions:
"Will this kill me?"
"Just how bad is chemo going to be?"
"How am I going to manage with 3 children and get through it all?"
"Will my cancer take me away from my life?"
"Will it make the quality of life I have left so bad I won't want to be here any more?"

All this and much more just sat here in this chair.
However, I am just one story.
How many more stories have begun from this chair?

The strange thing is, that, although it has been here where I have faced the toughest of news and the harshest of blows, this chair has held me up and supported me with its strong arms.

An interesting fact to me is that this chair is continuity for me and, when I next go to the hospital, I know at least one thing will be there to support me again, like it does for so many others.

CHAPTER 6

CONNECTION AND CONTRIBUTION

CONNECTION HELPS

Connection is such an important part of life. It's primal and it's powerful.
We're all part of the same thing – humanity, living life together.
We're all connected.
Connection is a gift. It gives hope, trust, a sense of worth.
The relationships we form and develop help bolster our strength.
They support us when life gets difficult.
They pull us out of dark places and one smile can reach our souls.
I feel grateful to be able to connect, not just with those closest to me;
my children, husband, friends and family, but also to people who
read the words that come out of my head onto the page.
Thank you for connecting with me.

Because connection helps.

Connection with family and friends and even strangers helps. All
of the roles I play involve other people – as a parent, I connect with
my children; as a wife, I connect with my husband. Friends, family
members, customers, blog readers, followers – there's a human
connection at the root of it all. And that helps.

One of the pillars of well-being is supportive relationships and I
have always found that supporting others is as comforting as feeling
supported. And yet, I have been blown away by the level of support
I have had from some. This has helped lift me up and I have found
that, through my writing, I have been able to connect with more
people than I thought possible.

Many years ago I heard the words, "You have cancer" for the first time.

I started recording and writing about my experiences as a wife and young mother of three, battling Non-Hodgkins lymphoma. I write about the full spectrum of emotions that I feel, including aimlessness, fear, despair, but also about the determination to always be strong with an enthusiasm and zest for life.

I have written about death, life, family, sadness, joy and sorrow. I thought my words would only appeal to people with cancer, but I was wrong. Incredibly the appeal has been far more universal and my words have stretched out into the world, further and further. I receive emails from people who, not only have or had cancer themselves, but also from those with family members who have had it.

I hear from people who have experience with other illnesses. I also receive emails from those who just want to know more about what it is like to confront mortality at an early age. The far-reaching emotional impact of illness affects many people, and they connect with my writing.

I now have stage 3B Non-Hodgkins cancer. I feel the need to communicate not only about the disease itself (true awareness) but also about its impact on my young family. My posts often show my insights into these beloved children of mine who are resilient and are coping with inevitable hardship.

I also hope to give a face and a voice to this disease through documenting my journey. I really want to help others. One way I am trying to help has been through setting up George Isaac satchels to raise money and through creating and sewing and making dolls and toys. Keeping myself busy as I do my best to help.

The blog (and this book) shall also be a record of my love and devotion to my children and my husband.

There is nowhere I would rather be than here with them. Nowhere but here. With them. And that is where my heart shall ALWAYS be.

Sometimes I close my eyes and imagine a perfect day with my husband and my children. A day where I am healthy. But then, when I hear the love in their voices and we laugh together, I mean actually crack up, I know that it is perfect, just them being there and me being here. With them.

I recommend journalling and visualising about your days and feelings and memories. Capture it all. The imagery, the sounds, the thoughts and emotions. Cameras, notepads, and within your heart. It all comes in useful on those days when you are wishing or wondering or waiting.

IT'S YOU I TREASURE

Writing a blog has been a lifeline for me. As well as enabling me to get my thoughts out of my head onto paper and out there into the world, it's been as rewarding as it's been cathartic. It's so exciting to see the readership grow. I've been busy reading the emails, tweets, and comments from readers who connect with what I've written in the hospital today. The notes of support and appeals to "keep doing what I'm doing" - they cheer me up.

When someone writes, "you've expressed what I'm feeling" or "I'm learning from you", it's just so moving and inspiring. I do try to answer emails, even if it's just a sentence or two, but sometimes I just cannot. And yet I read EVERY word that is written to me and hope those whom I cannot reply to individually forgive me.

I strive in my writing, not to just focus on cancer per se, but on the emotions of cancer ... the disease itself is not usually what's important. Instead, what I try to focus on are the emotions that accompany these hardships: fear, anger, despair, hope, grief, love.

At the moment, the side effects from the chemo have varied from annoying / challenging / painful, to quite tolerable. This is as much as I can hope for. I was able to spend a lot of time with my family and friends this last week and weekend, which was just so normal. Normality is beautiful.

I will continue with the dosing that I have done. Before starting the next round I do blood-work, make any adjustments to the dose based on tolerability of side effects, and repeat the process. I will do this as long as the cancer responds to the drug and does not spread further. I will be on some form of chemotherapy for the rest of my life.

I know there are so many of you reading these words who don't know me personally. But that doesn't matter. I understand how reading a diary of the inner-most thoughts of someone facing stage 3B lymphoma cancer brings us together. United as human beings, there is a connection that can be made.

I treasure all readers and supporters of my cause who have been with me, encouraging me from the start and love hearing from new readers too. Thanks to you all for reading. I appreciate all of the warm greetings I've had so far. They warm my heart.

Getting support from far and wide strengthens me. Like the support and strength I get from my family.

MY CHEERLEADERS: FRIENDSHIP AT 40

2015 has not been an easy year, with the cancer spreading, but it has had some mind-blowingly wonderful moments that I shall always cherish. I am here in AMERICA! Yes, I got to live my dream and travel to New York for my 40th birthday this Winter. It is so very beautiful – I am savouring every single moment!

And, while I am here, living a dream that I didn't think I would ever be able to fulfil, my dearest friends – my cheerleaders - collaborated by creating a montage of love and support for my birthday – to show me how much they care.

It touched me deeply as I logged on to Facebook to see the most overwhelming collage of amazing people! Needless to say, many a happy tear was shed! I literally felt so overwhelmed with this! When I woke up to this collection of pictures this morning, to see my friends' faces peering back at me, it didn't feel real. The effort from everyone with their art work was brilliant! It also shows how much of the world we cover, and how awesome and amazing Facebook is to enable us to do things like this and feel close together, no matter how far we are geographically from each other.

Thank you all so much!

You are all amazing and thank you so much to Cheryl for organising this special gift of love. I really don't know what to say. As I stand here in the land of the Americans about to head off to watch basket ball with my family, I feel so lucky for all that I have. I will treasure these pictures, you will never know how much you guys up lift me. Thank you! 🖤

My friends have really helped and supported me through this journey and I love them so much. Supportive relationships are so important in helping us deal with difficult times and I feel so blessed to have such caring, helpful and supportive friends.

THESE ARE THE DAYS I FOUGHT FOR

These last few weeks have been magical to me.
These were the days I fought for.
These were the days I wanted.
These are the days I longed to share with my husband and my children. And I am doing just that.

I've been overwhelmed with emotions in these weeks.
Spending this time with my children and being so proud of, not only what they do, but also who they are. They're amazing!

I think, when it comes down to it, I may have cancer, but I am blessed in so many ways.
Being alive to share these days with my friends and family.
My days are full and I do not take them for granted.
Thank you to all of you who have been there for me daily, loving and supporting; not only me, but my family too.
I couldn't do this without you.

Goodbye 2015.

As the sun sets, I have learned many new lessons. And I continue to feel so blessed with an AMAZING husband and children and friends. I wish all of you a happy and beautiful and peaceful New Year and may it bring you happiness x

TIME FLIES

Growing up fast
Standing tall
It's time to say goodbye to your Junior School
Don't look back
Look straight ahead
Time to move on
The world awaits
You held my hand tight
On your first day at school
But try as we might
The clock hands tick by
Time moves on for us all
Goodbye is near
Your class soon to scatter
Last hours together
Now it's the memories that matter
Goodbye Junior School
Thank you for all that's been learnt
George Francis now leaves with precious life skills earned.

As I work on the final pages of this book, my son George is in his 2nd year at senior school and my oldest two children have left school. Time has flown. The cancer is still with me. I've had treatment upon treatment and have had another operation this week. I've had long durations where I haven't been able to write at all and have had to stop running my satchel business, as I couldn't bear letting people down if I was too ill to fulfil orders. I've enjoyed making dolls instead – dolls with wigs for children who suffer from this same illness as me.

I can do this more flexibly than I could running a business. And I've put pen to paper when I can. I've also been away on another holiday. I didn't think I could or should, but my husband wouldn't take the children without me. And so summer 2016 has given me some precious happy moments. I'm so glad he persuaded me to go with them all.

OPENED UP

As I sit here looking out at the ocean, I am filled with a new sense of determination. I'm not ashamed to say I have had terrible depression and have felt quite mentally broken, and not just by my illness. I have felt like giving up, but, being in this beautiful place with my gorgeous family, I am going home ready to face it all again!

Thank you Croatia for your beauty, and thank you Mr Francis, Josh, Bethany, George, Jess Reynell and Maddy Coe.

ROOTS AND WINGS

"There are two lasting bequests
we can give our children: roots and wings,"

Hodding Carter

We lay the foundations for our children so they know where home is and we provide them with sufficient independence via wings with which to fly off with, to put what we've taught them into practice, and soar towards their dreams.

I am so thankful that I had my children when I did. I was the first of my friends to have children and thank goodness I did. They make me so happy, so content, so proud.

Today, my daughter is heading off again. I love watching her grow and enjoy life. Oh to be young and carefree. She amazes me and makes me so proud. This girl. And the relationship the three of them have comforts me. They're close and I know they'll take care of each other, always.

LAST DAY OF SENIOR SCHOOL

There are so many things I hope I've given you: skills, characteristics and traits to help you find your way in this world.

I hope I will have more years to watch you grow and see what you will do in the years ahead.

You make me proud, you make me smile, you make me laugh, Now, forever and always, I believe in you.

FATHER'S DAY

I knew I was lucky marrying Jonathan Francis, but when we took our vows, little did we know how much 'in sickness and in health' would mean. I just wouldn't cope without him! I really want to thank him and tell him how much I love him for everything he does for us. He works so very very hard and takes on so much without a moan or groan. He is not only my rock and my everything, but he is the BEST DAD!! Our children are so very lucky to have him as their father. Thank you Jonathan Francis for being our support and strength; we love you so very very much!

LEARNING HOW TO LIVE

"It always seems impossible until it's done,"

Nelson Mandela

I went in for an operation this week and it all went a bit pear-shaped. I ended up in intensive care with partial collapsed lungs on both sides. My heart rate rose dangerously high and it was all very dramatic. Thankfully, my heart rate was slowed down by lots of medicine and now it's back to a normal rhythm, so I'm just feeling a bit overwhelmed, sore and tired.

As I slip in and out of sleep, fond memories pop into my head. Laughter, the smell of flowers, the feeling of my childrens' soft cheeks on mine, my husband's eyes, friends, children I used to teach, people I used to know, songs I used to sing – the fabric of my life, the snapshots of living that I cherish.

And, on waking, I reflect on what matters and on what I have discovered about how to live. Here is what I have learned:

1. **Be kind. Always.** Even when someone says something that troubles you; even if someone is mean. Try hard to take the high road and respond with grace. Think about those you can help; those whose lives you could make a difference to; what strengths you have, which someone could benefit from

using or learning. Because we're all just muddling through and your kindness might be the only kindness a person experiences that day. Kindness is important, because it makes other people feel good and has the added benefit of making you feel good too.

2. **Remind yourself often about the majesty and beauty of nature and the sky.** When life gets difficult, whether fleetingly or permanently, nature can be such a tonic. I find the scent of a flower or looking up as I walk in the woods, has a calming and uplifting effect on me.

3. **Get a pet.** They lighten the mood. And they are (invariably) fluffy. Nobody ever had too much fluff in their life.

4. **It's possible to listen, even if you can't hear.** I wish I could hear again. But what I can do is lip-read and communicate via text and other technology. It's important to find out how people are doing and understand what is going on in their lives. I love the quote 'Listen to understand, not to reply.' Doing that definitely improves the connection between people. And if I can listen, even without being able to hear, anyone can and should.

5. **Don't be too hard on yourself.** I'm hard on myself, even now. I don't want to be a burden or let people down and I know I shouldn't be hard on myself, but sometimes I am. I think it's in our human nature to be judgemental and critical of ourselves, but I've realised we spend too much time doing that and no good comes from it. So give yourself a break.

SHE STOOD IN THE STORM

6. **Bad stuff happens that may be out of your control**. It does make you appreciate the good stuff when that happens (and it does) much more.

7. **Read more**. It can help you escape or learn, either are worthwhile endeavours for the soul.

8. **Get outdoors as often as you can.** Breathe in the fresh air and soak up the sun or splash in the rain.

9. **Appreciate people more than things.** Love is a powerful healing feeling. Connecting with people is a gift. People generate feelings, whether good or bad, and to feel is to live. So be grateful for people in your life who make you feel.

10. **Savour moments.** Capture them. Reminisce often. But most importantly, soak up every little drop of right now.

11. **Press pause.** When life gets too busy to have any downtime, that's probably the time when you need some downtime the most. You owe it to yourself and your loved ones to prioritise you from time to time. Life is for living, so take care of you! Because life is waiting for you to pause enough to enjoy it.

LIVING LIFE

I think about the sentence that changed my life.

I think of where I've been, where I am, where I am going.

I think of those I've met along the way: new friends, doctors, nurses, strangers.

I think of those who have died from cancer and other causes since I was diagnosed.

I think of the progress we've made and the distance we have yet to go.

I think of what today might bring, and tomorrow.

And then, in a sudden reversal, I stop myself from thinking too much. "It's time to go live my life," I tell myself. Thinking is good, but only so much.

"It's time to go live my life," I tell myself.

And so I shall.

I wish you all the very best in living yours.

Printed in Great Britain
by Amazon